IOANNIS VASILEIOU

EUROPEAN UNION BUDGET

*ISSUES ABOUT THE ALLOCATION
AND REDISTRIBUTION OF RESOURCES
IN THE EUROPEAN UNION*

ATHENS 2018

PUBLISHED IN GREEK BY HISTORICAL QUEST IN 2017

TRANSLATED INTO ENGLISH IN 2018

TRANSLATED BY THE AUTHOR HIMSELF

ART DIRECTOR: SOFIA LIVIERATOU

ACKNOWLEDGEMENTS
To my beloved Maria Nikou for her
encouragement and moral support

TABLE OF CONTENTS

<u>INTRODUCTION</u>

The European Union (EU) budget can effectively be regarded as a first-class compass for the satisfactory funding of all individual policies. Its detailed study provides adequate information on specific EU problems and needs, which precisely determine the expenditure percentage. Through the budget's meticulous scrutiny, the particular noteworthiness of certain individual initiatives and activities, combined with the degree of success regarding past policies can be sufficiently demonstrated.

Generally speaking, the foremost revenue sources are three. The first is a percentage, often approximately 0.7% of the Gross National Income (GNI) of every member state. Nonetheless, it is stressed that if such a contribution results in tribulations for other states, suitable adjustments indeed take place (Europa/How the EU is funded, 2017).

The second source is a rate of around 0.3% of revenue from the harmonized Value Added Tax (VAT) of each country, while the third is a fairly high rate of import duties imposed on products from third countries[1] (Europa/How the EU is funded, 2017).

At the same time, the Union receives a) contributions from third countries to EU programs, b) taxes on EU staff salaries and c) fines imposed to companies that violate EU rules (Europa/ How the EU is funded, 2017).

---

1. *The country collecting the duty withholds a small percentage.*

We also underline the fact that member states reach agreements not only regarding the European budget size but also on the exact method it will be financed numerous years in advance. Moreover, special emphasis is placed on the fact that the Union's budget efficaciously contributes towards the rapid confrontation regarding the scourge of unemployment, due to the fact that it ceaselessly promotes growth and enhances the creation of new jobs, which is an infinitely pivotal priority in the difficult times we are experiencing (Europa/How the EU is funded, 2017).

Concurrently, the Union's budget systematically supports European rural areas' efficient development, while it also funds investment in order for economic disparities between states and regions within the Union to be reduced, in the broader framework of cohesion policy (Europa/How the EU is funded, 2017).

As we will see in the following chapters, the budget is not only available within the EU but also outside. This implies both its magnitude and the Union's noteworthiness in the context of international developments. The budget's significance becomes even greater if the general sociopolitical instability at a global level is taken into account.

For 2015, 87% of the funds were earmarked for "Smart and inclusive growth" and "Sustainable growth: natural resources". These are also the focal initiatives, in need of further analysis as they deeply influence both the Union's present and future planning.

The dominant purpose of this study is to serve as an efficacious and accessible guide for a constructive interpretation of EU budget.

We surely acknowledge the immense complexity of budget policies and therefore we systematically attempt to provide a simplified scientific view, but without omitting fundamental details.

This book comprises four chapters. In Chapter 1, "*A Brief Historical Overview*" is critically being presented and the most important political events, as well as the major alterations that affected EU budget from the 1960s onwards are being meticulously scrutinized.

Discussions and decisions on the "Integrated Mediterranean Programmes", the Common Agricultural Policy (CAP) and issues relating to budget revenue and trade balance of certain member states are being scrupulously analyzed.

Concomitantly, the role and cooperation between the foremost institutions, the Fontainebleau European Council, the remarkable Interinstitutional Agreement of 1988, the exceptional attitude of British Prime Minister Margaret Thatcher during the 1980s, as well as the entire range of efforts to combat risks incurred by the outbreak of international financial crisis in 2008 are being painstakingly examined.

In Chapter 2, we focus on *"EU Budget Setting - up and Magnitude"*. The principal aim is for the reader to become familiar with a) the exact method according to which the budget is drawn-up, b) its significance, and c) its general characteristics. Additionally, we attempt to satisfactory elucidate key budgetary terms, namely the Multiannual Financial Framework (MFF), the "own resources" and the "discharge" concept.Simultaneously, within this chapter, the multifarious role of the European Parliament, the Council of the

EU, the European Commission, the European Economic and Social Committee, the Committee of the Regions, the European Court of Auditors (ECA), the European Ombudsman and the Eurogroup, as far as budget policies are concerned, is being critically discussed.

The spectrum of bodies and committees actively involved in the process is irrefutably vast and the committees examined perform highly specialized roles. The entire range of activities is outstandingly complex, but we remain optimistic that our analysis can facilitate the reader to identify with both the functions and the general philosophy of the Union.

In Chapter 3, we concentrate on *"EU Budget Allocation"*, which is an issue of paramount significance especially these days. Apart from providing a detailed breakdown, particular reference is made to a number of fundamental programs and mechanisms funded by the Union budget, namely "Horizon 2020", "Human Brain", the "Business Development Centre" at the Letterkenny Institute of Technology, the European Progress Microfinance Facility, the joint EU and UNICEF project, LIFE, RAPEX, MEDIA, COSME, Connecting Europe Facility, Erasmus +, the "Youth Employment Initiative", the Development Cooperation Instrument (DCI), the "European Neighborhood Instrument", the Instrument for Pre-Accession Assistance, the Asylum, Migration and Integration Fund and the Internal Security Fund.

In Chapter 4, the foremost *"Concluding Remarks"* are being drawn and up-to-date developments regarding EU budget policies and activities are being summarized. An attempt to calculate the success rate thus far takes place and this is accompanied by a methodical focus on future perspectives.

It is essential to stress that the present fluidity prohibits long-term forecasts, which we deliberately avoid. Time is always the only (and relentless) judge, but this does not negate the fact that the EU has already succeeded in achieving a satisfactory budgetary distribution.

CHAPTER 1

A BRIEF HISTORICAL OVERVIEW

The fundamental pursuit of this chapter is the provision of an epigrammatic historical overview, in order for the most noteworthy events that have occasionally affected EU budget to be critically highlighted. History teaches and is often repeated, so its knowledge is absolutely indispensable.

Deliberately, we avoid entering into a vast amount of details, since our precise objective is to provide the reader with a general picture in a straightforward and graspable way. Besides, we remain optimistic that the bibliography is sufficient enough for all those wishing to perform a deeper scrutiny in the context of historical events.

EU budget has been existing since 1967, following the union of two separate budgets established by the Treaty of Rome in 1957 to respectively cover the costs of both the Commission of the European Communities and the European Atomic Energy Community (Cipriani, 2014; Matthijs, 2010; Seremetis, 1995; Vasileiou, 2013a, 2013b, 2014a, 2014b, 2015 and 2017).

Initially, budget revenues came from member states' contributions, but during the 1970s, a significant alteration took place and the budget actually acquired its own revenues.

These are collected from member states' budgets and are then attributed to the Union. At that particular time the various interventions of the Union's budget, financed by specific expenditure, were significally expanded (Cipriani, 2014; Matthijs, 2010; Seremetis, 1995; Vasileiou, 2013a, 2013b, 2014a, 2014b, 2015 and 2017).

It is also indicated that over the years, remarkable community appropriations were sufficiently programmed, while community regulations for "Integrated Mediterranean Programmes", education, transport and the environment were also approved (Cipriani, 2014; Matthijs, 2010; Seremetis, 1995; Vasileiou, 2013a, 2013b, 2014a, 2014b, 2015 and 2017).

Additionally, a) the highly significant establishment of the "own resources", b) the functional expansion regarding its spending and c) the efficacious strengthening of jurisdictions of Community institutions and bodies which prepare and implement it, provided the Union's budget with a certain form of autonomy if compared to its original dimension which was based on member states' ad hoc consensus (Cipriani, 2014; Matthijs, 2010; Núñez Ferrer, 2007; Seremetis, 1995).

This autonomy, albeit somewhat limited, was probably inevitable but also essential for a more rational serving of the Union's interests towards a brighter future. We must also add that the own resources were established in 1970, replacing the member states' contributions (Cipriani, 2014; Matthijs, 2010; Núñez Ferrer, 2007; Seremetis, 1995).

Predominantly until the end of the 1980s, EU budget was somehow accused of stiffness and stagnation, while quite a lot of complaints existed in the context of issues such as a) the large sums for the CAP, b) inadequate budget revenue and c) the negative balance of transactions of some member states (Cipriani, 2014; Matthijs, 2010; Nugent, 2012; Seremetis, 1995; Vasileiou, 2013a, 2013b, 2014a, 2014b, 2015 and 2017).

As a matter of fact, principally in the beginning of the 1980s, budgetary crises were commonplace within the Union and this inevitably had a serious impact on the budget. Furthermore, the three chief institutions (Parliament, Council and Commission) were in constant friction, which in some cases took the form of political bickering (Cipriani, 2014; Matthijs, 2010; Nugent, 2012; Núñez Ferrer, 2007; Seremetis, 1995; Vasileiou, 2013a, 2013b, 2014a, 2014b, 2015 and 2017).

Without exaggeration, at that particular time the Parliament was a bit disturbed, not only due to a fund deficit regarding expenditure outside CAP, but also because of a certain number of restrictions in the wider context of its budgetary powers (Cipriani, 2014; Matthijs, 2010; Nugent, 2012; Núñez Ferrer, 2007; Seremetis, 1995; Vasileiou, 2013a, 2013b, 2014a, 2014b, 2015 and 2017).

It is only natural, in the context of a political or economic union, for disputes to appear in terms of economic issues and even more so while speaking about the (then) European Economic Community (EEC), which comprised some of the most economically advanced states worldwide.

And of course, we must not ignore that usually powerful member states are rather displeased when they believe they play a minor role in political affairs compared to others. In such cases, the EEC was called upon to reconcile situations.

Moreover, during the 1980s, Thatcher had actually engaged herself in a constant struggle in order to achieve the decrease of Great Britain's net contributions to the budget, as she regarded them as excessive (Cipriani, 2014; Matthijs, 2010; Nugent, 2012).

In 1984, a pivotal agreement on the budget at the European Council in Fontainebleau in France (about 55 kilometers southeast of Paris) became a reality. This actually focused on a number of innovative fiscal discipline rules, the reduction of Great Britain contributions and the increase of resources with a VAT cap of 1.4% from 1986 (Cipriani, 2014; Matthijs, 2010; Nugent, 2012).

Nevertheless, we strongly believe that the abovementioned agreement failed to result in radical solutions to general problems and budget disagreements. It was unambiguous that more direct and deeper cuts to combat protracted fiscal difficulties were essential.

The Interinstitutional Agreement of 1988 was indeed a worthwhile initiative, due to the fact that it led to the significant multiannual financial perspectives of 1988-92, which indubitably gave the Union budget new impetus and entity (Cipriani, 2014; Matthijs, 2010; Nugent, 2012; Núñez Ferrer, 2007; Seremetis, 1995).

In the context of the aforesaid agreement, all three institutions committed themselves to the abovementioned financial perspectives, which aimed towards a) the establishment of a new and perhaps even more functional framework concerning fiscal discipline, b) the increase of resources via a new financial source based on the Gross Domestic Product (GDP) of each country, c) the coveted, yet problematic reduction regarding CAP expenditures and d) the decrease of British contributions. Since 1988, all the Union's annual budgets have been adopted within the MFF[2] (Cipriani, 2014; Matthijs, 2010; Nugent, 2012; Núñez Ferrer, 2007; Seremetis, 1995).

In 2008, when the calamitous economic and financial crisis broke out internationally, member states managed to realize all immediate risks that had arisen. As expected, national governments, the Commission, as well as the European Central Bank (ECB) were rapidly mobilized against a treacherous enemy, the full impact of which was utterly impossible to be predicted at that precise moment (Europa/Money and the EU, 2017; Vasileiou, 2013a, 2013b, 2014a, 2014b, 2015 and 2017).

It is worth underlining the deep and profound cooperation of the abovementioned parties in the context of a) the effective protection of deposits, b) the direct promotion of employment and growth (to the extent that this was actually realistic at that particular era), c) financial stability, d) the unremitting

---

2. *We must note that MFFs used to be called "financial perspectives" until their entry into the Treaties. With the Treaty of Lisbon, they officially received the name MFF.*

preservation in terms of the availability of affordable borrowing for both households and businesses and e) the functional implementation of a more efficient governance system in the future (Europa/Money and the EU, 2017; Vasileiou, 2013a, 2013b, 2014a, 2014b, 2015 and 2017).

Analyzing the events of the past and, concomitantly, taking the current situation into consideration, we acknowledge that the budget can irrefutably be regarded as the Union's "backbone", since its set-up is the driving force behind the entire spectrum of strategies. Therefore, a meticulous scrutiny regarding budget distribution is imperative, in order for any dark points to be adequately elucidated.

In the following chapter, we attempt to methodically analyze the Union's budget setting-up, as well as its incontestable magnitude.

The entire range of its foremost procedures are scrupulously examined and evaluated, while the particularly complex role of the European Parliament, the Council of the EU, the European Commission, the European Economic and Social Committee, the Committee of the Regions, the ECA and the European Ombudsman is also depicted in detail.

Special emphasis is placed on EUs truly admirable coordination, which is a remarkable achievement, due to the fact that it manages to successfully deal with an enormous variety of institutions and committees, characterized by particularly complex functions and increased responsibilities. It goes without saying that serving the general interest always remains the primary target.

Our hitherto conducted research leads us to the conclusion that transparency, accuracy, immediacy in political decisions and the pursuit of maximum efficiency, combined with top-class sophistication in planning, are instantly recognizable features of EU mechanisms. Any errors, especially these days, may prove to be fatal and the Union is well aware of this.

CHAPTER 2

EU BUDGET SETTING-UP AND MAGNITUDE

The Union's annual budget is one of the three components of its budgetary system. The other two are a) the MFF, which is responsible for setting expenditure limits (ceilings) for a number of years and b) the own resources' rules which practically establish the Union's revenue (European Council/Council of the European Union/Budget, 2016).

In particular, the annual budget includes all EU revenue and expenditure for one year and we must underline that it also guarantees the adequate financing of Union actions and programs in the entire spectrum of its policy areas. What is more, it ensures that the Union receives the necessary revenue to sufficiently finance its expenditure. It is obvious that the annual budget must be balanced, otherwise serious tribulations arise (European Council/Council of the European Union/Budget, 2016).

Legislation on the budget is laid down in Articles 310-324 (budget) of the Treaty on the Functioning of the EU (Europa/ Budget, 2017).

In the context of this book, it is highlighted that the budget is subject to specific limits. These are precisely defined by the MFF, which sets the maximum annual amounts that the Union can spend on policies in a given period, usually seven years. For all intents and purposes, the MFF is responsible for effectively setting the maximum annual expenditure limits of the Union (the so-called "ceilings") in numerous policy areas, known as "headings". It is essential to mention that within each budget area (heading), funding is provided either via funds or programs (Europa/Budget, 2017; European Commission/Budget, 2014). We undeniably acknowledge the MFF's enormous notability, since it can actually be regarded as the budget's guiding principle.

As regards the Union's expenditure, both long-term priorities and constraints are precisely defined in the MFF. The Commission, the Parliament and the Council are involved not only in determining the budget size, but also in the method of allocating expenditure. The Commission is in charge of expenditures (Europa/How the EU budget is spent, 2017).

The budget is adopted on an annual basis. The Commission prepares the draft budget and submits it to the Parliament and the Council, which form the so-called "budgetary authority". The draft is then amended and approved by both institutions (Council and Parliament) (Europa/Budget, 2017; European Commission/Budget, 2014).

In case of a disagreement between the Council and the Parliament, a special conciliation committee is convened with the aim of reaching an agreement on a joint text within 21 days.

If the Council rejects the joint text, the Parliament has the right to ultimately approve the budget. If the joint text is rejected by the Parliament, the Commission is obliged to submit a new draft budget (Europa/Budget, 2017; European Commission/Budget, 2014).

We note in particular that unless the budget is adopted before the beginning of the new year, one twelfth of the budget of the previous year may be spent each month under specified conditions before the final agreement on the new budget. The Commission is charged with the ultimate responsibility regarding budget implementation (Europa/Budget, 2017; European Commission/Budget, 2014).

Almost 80% of Union funds are actually spent together with member states under the shared management context, where expenditure is not managed by the Commission but by member state authorities under the Commission's supervision (Europa/Budget, 2017; European Commission/Budget, 2014).

We acknowledge that the whole procedure is transparent and this element unquestionably gives increased credibility to the EU decision process. Such a method is incontestably useful to the Union itself, should we take the enormous degree of complicatedness into consideration. Concomitantly, it inspires a sense of trust in the citizens who feel they are not deceived.

At the beginning of each new MFF period, all member states without a single exception have to take decisions (by consensus), as regards both the type, and the maximum amounts of own resources the Union can raise during a year, as well as the exact way they will be calculated (Europa/Budget, 2017; Europa/How the EU is funded, 2017; European Commission/Budget, 2014).

This is the absolutely vital "own resources decision". In summary, the member states' target is the agreement (with a sovereign decision) to ensure a certain revenue level to the Union budget over the entire period and its conversion into common EU own resources (Europa/Budget, 2017; Europa/How the EU is funded, 2017; European Commission/Budget, 2014).

Own resources can be broken down as follows: a) traditional own resources, which are customs duties on imports from non-EU countries and sugar levies (under the MFF 2007-13, member states retained 25% of these amounts in order to adequately cover collection costs), b) own resources based on GNI, which means that there is a transfer of a certain percentage of the "wealth" of each member state in the Union budget (for 2013, this was 0.84321% of GNI, while it is highlighted that this system is the most significant revenue source of EU budget and in 2013 accounted to 73.8% of total revenue) and c) own resources based on VAT (a uniform rate of 0.3% applied with certain exceptions to member states' harmonized VAT base) (Europa/How the EU is funded, 2017; European Commission/Budget, 2014).

Miscellaneous revenue sources which reached approximately 5.8% in 2013 include a) bank interest, b) tax and other deductions from the Union's staff remunerations, c) interest on late payments, d) fines and e) non-EU countries contributions in the context of specific programs (Europa/How the EU is funded, 2017; European Commission/Budget, 2014). In terms of each year's budget, the amounts agreed in advance (based on the MFF) are clearly set. The MFF generally enables the Union to proceed with the planning of funding programs for numerous years in advance. The current MFF covers the 2014-20 period. It is also essential to add that the Commission has the ultimate responsibility for budget allocation, but approximately 80% of EU funds are being managed by national governments. This is a critical detail which under no circumstances must go unnoticed (Europa/How the EU budget is spent, 2017).

In the case of undue payments, the Commission cooperates in a systematic manner with the member states concerned so as for the money to be recovered. Special emphasis is placed on the fact that in order to ensure further transparency, both companies and organizations receiving EU funding are on public record. This is another characteristic example of the Union's intensified efforts to unremittingly promote the concept of good governance and efficient management within the entire range of its policies (Europa/How the EU budget is spent, 2017).

As far as expenditure is concerned, it is divided into payments ("payment appropriations" if we would like to be more precise) and commitments (or "commitment appropriations"). Payments cover expenditure due in the current year and clearly arise from legal commitments entered into in the current year and/or previous years. Commitments cover the legal obligations' entire cost that could be signed in a given financial year. In particular, legal obligations may be grant agreements, contracts and decisions (European Council/Council of the European Union/ Budget, 2016).

A few more salient issues need to be clarified for a more coherent understanding: a) both commitments and payments are equal for the expenditure that is obligatory to be made in the same year, b) the amounts of payments and commitments usually differ in terms of multiannual projects[3], c) it is necessary for the expenditure side of the Union's annual budget to remain within the expenditure limits (ceilings) set in MFF[4] and d) the amount committed but not yet paid out to beneficiaries is named "outstanding commitments" (European Council/Council of the European Union/Budget, 2016).

In the context of the Union's annual budget, a special section (Section II) on the shared budget of the European Council and the Council of the EU is included. Our hitherto conducted research enables us to conclude that the budget of the Council and the European Council is sufficiently managed by the General Secretariat of the Council of the EU (European Council/Council of the European Union/Budget, 2016).

According to 2015 figures, the annual budget of the Union

---

3. *In this case, the commitment appropriations would be made in one year, but the payment appropriations would actually be divided into smaller amounts to be paid over a number of years.*

4. *Normally, the Union sets its annual budget at a lower level compared to the expenditure ceilings established in the MFF regulation, in order to be capable of adequately covering unexpected expenditure wherever necessary.*

is €145 bn, but it is worth noting that this figure corresponds to only 1% of the member states' wealth produced per year. In particular, at present, the EU budget accounts for approximately 1% of the Union's GNI, but the national budgets of EU member states constitute almost 49% (Europa/Budget, 2017; European Commission/Budget, 2014).

At this point, it is worth highlighting a number of details that largely concentrate on the general philosophy regarding EU budget. First and foremost, the Union budget is mainly regarded as an "investment budget", since its concern is to effectively pool resources from member states with a view to creating economies of scale. It finances activities that member states can fund more rationally through cooperation, notably in the outstandingly neuralgic fields of research, climate change, information and communication technologies, energy and transport (Europa/Budget, 2017; European Commission/Budget, 2014).

Concurrently, as far as a number of countries are concerned, EU budget is the only (without exaggeration) source for investment in terms of the particularly challenging infrastructure sector. EU budget supports and funds certain investment projects that could otherwise not be carried out, while it can also be used to guarantee loans to member states with economic problems (Europa/Budget, 2017; European Commission/Budget, 2014).

We also underline that these guarantees can indeed have significant multiplier effects. This means for example that one euro guaranteed by the Union budget could actually represent up to €12 raised by a small or medium-sized enterprise (SME). Finally, it is important to mention that the Union budget does not fund either social protection or defense expenditure, nor does it provide funds for police work or schools' running. Such a detail must be seriously taken into consideration (Europa/Budget, 2017; European Commission/Budget, 2014).

One of the most critical questions is the method by which money control is carried out. It is unambiguous that the current economic downturn dictates a strict and scrupulous investigation process in terms of spending, in order for any kind of fraud or mismanagement to be avoided (Europa/Budget, 2017; European Commission/Budget, 2014).

The Union budget is controlled by specific bodies and governed by certain rules. The foremost rules on the Union's actual spending can be discovered in its financial regulation. Additionally, application rules explain the correct methods according to which financial regulation is to be applied. It is particularly stressed that rules are often not only re-examined but also simplified in the most effective way to maximize, inter alia, the facilitation of small beneficiaries (Europa/Budget, 2017; European Commission/Budget, 2014).

The Union's budget is subject to both external and internal audits, with the main aim of guaranteeing the widest possible transparency, which always leads to increased solvency. If the Commission discovers that EU budget money was unduly paid, it is absolutely essential to ensure its recovery in an effective and immediate manner

(Europa/Budget, 2017; European Commission/Budget, 2014).

Moreover, a significant independent external audit takes place annually by the ECA, in the context of the Union's annual accounts. Particular emphasis is placed on member states' equal responsibility in terms of the overall transparency, support and protection as far as the Union's financial interests are concerned (Europa/Budget, 2017; European Commission/Budget, 2014).

When errors are detected, they can be immediately corrected before the payment is made, but we must add that corrections can also be applied to final payments, since the majority of EU projects run over for more than a year. In such cases, the initial amounts granted are reimbursed to the Commission, unless an alternative proposal is submitted in time by member states. Using this particular method, in 2013, the Commission effectively managed to correct, or recover €3.3 bn, which is indeed a fairly high number (Europa/Budget, 2017; European Commission/ Budget, 2014).

Apart from that, possible fraud cases are meticulously scrutinized by the European Anti-Fraud Office (OLAF). We have to mention, however, that these cases concern only approximately 0.2% of the budget. Based on the ECA's annual report, the Parliament and the Council evaluate the Union budget implementation. The Parliament then decides whether or not to grant discharge to the Commission (Europa/Budget, 2017; European Commission/Budget, 2014).

It is precisely the concept of "discharge" which is of crucial importance, as it means the approval of the manner according to which the Commission has implemented the budget in the financial year in question and the closure of that budget (Europa/Budget, 2017; European Commission/Budget, 2014).

We certainly acknowledge the fact that the process is simple, functional and transparent so, at least as far as we are concerned, there is no room for deliberate malfunctioning. Undeniably, the Union's fundamental principle has always been the service of general interest within the entire spectrum of its strategies and policies.

As a consequence, as far as the budget issue is concerned, the benchmark remains unchanged, which means that the budget use focuses precisely on what is essential for the overall benefit, such as a) substantially strengthening the European economy competitiveness at international level, b) a more effective environmental protection at European level, c) more functional connections in the neuralgic energy, transport and communications sectors between member states and d) incentives and assistance in general to European researchers and scientists, aiming towards the efficient joining of their skills and capabilities beyond their national borders to successfully establish a "Pan-European" scientific community (Europa/Budget, 2017).

Such a community, if governed by rational cooperation and planning, is capable of performing titanic research and training, offering more than a few radical solutions to the severe thorny economic and sociopolitical problems of the present era.

Budget-related policies' implementation must be characterized by well-functioning cooperation and excellent coordination between institutions. The budget's momentousness is such that an efficient participation of a multitude of committees, performing different roles but with common components is unquestionably required.

In the previous paragraphs, the role of a number of the principal bodies and committees relating to EU budget policies and strategies was briefly examined. A more detailed analysis of the specific roles of the European Parliament, the Council of the EU, the European Commission, the European Economic and Social Committee, the Committee of the Regions, the ECA and the European Ombudsman is therefore necessary.

Two European Parliament committees are involved in the budget. The first is the Committee on Budgets (BUDG) and the second the Committee on Budgetary Control (CONT). BUDG comprises 41 full members and as many substitutes, while its pursuit is the systematic discussion, amendment and adoption of the Union's budget together with the Council of Ministers (European Parliament/Committees/Budgets, 2017).

In terms of the current parliamentary term, CONT consists of 30 members from 17 member states. As a rule, parliamentary committees meet once or twice a month. The aim is to thoroughly control the use of Union budget resources. We have to add that the European Commission manages most of the budget and spends 80% in member states, almost 13% in other parts of the world and around 7% in administration (European Parliament/Committees/Budgetary Control, 2017).

CONT systematically investigates the use of resources and whether specific policy objectives are being successfully implemented. It also examines in detail whether Union citizens receive real added value for the price they pay (European Parliament/Committees/Budgetary Control, 2017).

Apart from that, CONT reports on both OLAF and the European Investment Bank, while it is actively involved in the so-called "cross-cutting" aspects of European legislation. We particularly underline that ECA reports are of significant assistance to CONT's work (European Parliament/Committees/Budgetary Control, 2017).

The Economic and Financial Affairs Council (Ecofin) is considered to be one of the most critical components in terms of budgetary policies, since it is responsible for economic policy, financial services' regulation, as well as taxation issues. It deals with financial markets, capital movements and economic relations with non-EU countries (European Council/Council of the European Union/Ecofin, 2017).

Moreover, it prepares the Union's annual budget and effectively deals with the euro's practical and legal aspects. It is also in charge of the proper coordination of member states' economic policies, the close monitoring of their budgetary policies and the effective promotion of their economic performance convergence (European Council/Council of the European Union/Ecofin, 2017).

Additionally, it is responsible for the financial aspects of international negotiations on measures to rationally tackle the scourge of climate change and is also in charge of the effective coordination of the Union's positions with regard to (particularly critical) international meetings, such as those in the context of G20, the World Bank and the International Monetary Fund (European Council/Council of the European Union/Ecofin, 2017).

The Ecofin Council consists of ministers of economics and finance of all member states, while particular emphasis must be placed on the fact that relevant European Commissioners also take part in the meetings. Apart from that, specific Ecofin sessions involving both ministers responsible for national budgets and the European Commissioner responsible for financial programming and budget take place, with a view to satisfactorily preparing the Union's annual budget. As a rule, Ecofin meets once a month (European Council/Council of the European Union/Ecofin, 2017).

It goes without saying that the Council of the EU is also of fundamental significance, due to the fact that it a) adopts the Union's annual budget together with the European Parliament, in accordance with a specific legislative procedure on the basis of a Commission proposal, b) has the power to amend the adopted annual budget together with the Parliament again on the basis of a Commission proposal and c) recommends to the Parliament whether the Commission should be granted discharge in respect of the EU annual budget implementation (European Council/

Council of the European Union/Budget, 2016).

What is more, the EU Council takes the final decision on the integration of a state into the euro area, on the basis of a Commission proposal and following the European Parliament's opinion (European Council/Council of the European Union/ Eurogroup, 2016).

The Eurogroup is an informal body where ministers of the euro area member states hold debates on issues relating to their shared responsibilities for the euro. The main concern is to ensure a close and functional coordination of economic policies between member states of the euro area, while simultaneously supporting and promoting economic growth and development. Furthermore, it is responsible for both the excellent preparation of the Euro Summit meetings, as well as their follow-up (European Council/ Council of the European Union/Eurogroup, 2016).

Normally, the Eurogroup meets once a month, on the eve of the Council Ecofin meeting. In the context of Eurogroup meetings, both the ECB president and the commissioner for economic and financial affairs, taxation and customs take part. On June 4, 1998, at the Château de Senningen in Luxembourg, the first informal meeting of finance ministers of the euro area members was held (European Council/Council of the European Union/ Eurogroup, 2016).

Moreover, every six months, the Eurogroup adopts its work program, which sets out in a precise manner the foremost areas of interest, while clearly identifying preliminary agendas regarding its following meetings. We must add that the Eurogroup elects its president for a 2.5-year term by a simple majority of votes (European Council/Council of the European Union/Eurogroup, 2016).

As far as the European Commission is concerned, we specifically focus on the enormously significant role played by both OLAF and the Internal Audit Service. OLAF is a priceless component in terms of the Union's ceaseless fight against all forms of fraud. Its task is the scrupulous investigation regarding cases of fraud against the Union's budget, which is a truly gigantic mission. OLAF attempts to discover any form of corruption or severe misconduct as far as the European institutions are concerned. Additionally, it is responsible for the successful establishment and advancement of the Commission's policy against fraud (OLAF, 2017).

Criminal offenses investigated by OLAF may include fraudulent claims, misappropriations, misconduct in public procurement procedures, customs fraud, as well as embezzlement. At this point, the magnitude of Hercule programs must be adequately highlighted. These programs are widely considered to be of vital noteworthiness since they manage to successfully fund actions to prevent and combat all forms of corruption, fraud, as well as miscellaneous illegal procedures and actions that are highly probable to result in serious tribulations in terms of the Union's financial interests (OLAF, 2017).

It is imperative to mention that actions funded by Hercule programs may be operational and technical support for investigation, specialized trainings and research activities. All these actions are effectively carried out through contracts and grants (OLAF, 2017). In other words, we irrefutably witness an excellent planning and organization, accompanied by the typical EU will to uncompromisingly stamp out any illegal practice as soon as possible.

It goes without saying that OLAF's work is truly admirable, since over the period 2010-15 it has managed to a) issue more than 1,600 recommendations for financial, administrative, judicial and disciplinary action to be taken by the competent authorities of both the EU and member states, b) bring to fruition over 1,400 investigations and c) recommend the recovery of more than €3 bn to the Union's budget (OLAF, 2017).

The Internal Audit Service (IAS) is also a component of paramount significance, due to the fact that it provides independent opinions, advice and recommendations concerning the quality and operation of internal control systems within the Commission, the Union agencies and other autonomous bodies (Internal Audit Service, 2017).

We fully acknowledge the noteworthiness of these competencies, since internal control is a critical factor in terms of an efficacious operation. Any possible disturbances will indubitably lead to a disruption of the Union's policy mechanism, with unforeseen consequences.

In summary, the IAS a) carries out approximately 150 audits per year in the various Commission departments, b) makes recommendations to the abovementioned departments on methods, according to which certain management procedures for control, risk and governance issues can be substantially improved, c) meticulously audits European institutions and other bodies receiving funding from the Union's budget and d) functionally promotes the fostering of sound and efficient management in Commission departments (Internal Audit Service, 2017).

The IAS's foremost plans and reports are a) the management plan, in which objectives, resources and activities are being scrupulously analyzed, b) the strategic plan explaining in detail the strategy and the targets of the department for the period 2016-20, c) the activity report, which reflects not only the objectives attained, but also initiatives and resources used during the year, and d) the annual report which effectively summarizes the outcome of IAS audits, recommendations and actions taken (Internal Audit Service, 2017).

In terms of the budget, a key role is also played by a) the Section for Economic and Monetary Union and Economic and Social Cohesion (ECO) of the European Economic and Social Committee and b) the Commission for Economic Policy (ECON) of the Committee of the Regions (European Economic and Social Committee, 2017). The ECO Section is responsible for a) economic and monetary policy coordination, b) the stability and growth pact, c) the broad economic policy guidelines, d) the euro area enlargement and e) miscellaneous issues relating to economic governance (European Economic and Social Committee, 2017).

Furthermore, the ECO Section responsibilities cover a) financial perspectives, b) own resources and the Union's budget and c) statistical questions. As far as taxation is concerned, the Section is in charge of efficiently addressing issues related to the particular neuralgic tax harmonization, as well as the approximation of laws (European Economic and Social Committee, 2017).

What is more, it successfully tackles burning issues concerning financial and capital markets and their integration, while within the particularly decisive field of economic and social cohesion its responsibilities include regional, structural and cohesion policy. Finally, the Section is responsible for spatial planning, urban policy and metropolitan areas (European Economic and Social Committee, 2017).

ECON is in charge of the best possible coordination in terms of the Committee of the Regions' work in the following areas: a) Economic and monetary policy, b) Economic Governance, European Semester, c) Industrial Policy, d) Internal market, e) International trade and tariffs, f) SME policy and g) Competition and State aid policy (CoR Commissions, 2017).

At this point, the fundamental role of the ECA in terms of the budget will be conscientiously examined. Generally speaking, the ECA can be regarded as the guardian of the Union's finances, since it has been set up to pursue the best possible financial auditing (European Court of Auditors, 2017).

We particularly highlight the fact that its audit work is based on the Union's budget and policies, with emphasis on the following areas: a) public finances, b) added value, c) growth and employment, and d) environment and climate action. We underline that the budget is audited by the ECA in terms not only of revenue but also spending (European Court of Auditors, 2017).

In summary, ECA's objectives are the following four: a) the sufficient improvement in terms of public accountability in the Union, b) the provision of satisfactory reports not only for citizens, but also for policy-makers, c) the closest possible cooperation with other top-class audit institutions and d) the successful setting of standards in the context of public finance audit (European Court of Auditors, 2017).

As far as the first objective is concerned, the results of ECA's work are being used in an operational manner by the European Parliament, the European Commission, the Council and member states not only for supervising the Union's budget management, but also for possible improvements (European Court of Auditors, 2017).

The ECA's particular notability is perfectly illustrated by the fact that its work is a central component regarding the annual discharge. This is an outstandingly significant procedure whereby the Parliament decides upon a Council recommendation if the Commission has been able to properly implement the previous financial year's budget. In the context of the second objective, we stress that ECA publications include special reports, annual reports, specific annual reports, position papers and opinions (European Court of Auditors, 2017).

The third objective focuses on the fact that up to 80% of the Union's budget management is actually shared with member states. The latter effectively cooperate with the Commission for the successful establishment of internal control and supervisory systems, so as to guarantee that Union funds are appropriately spent. We argue that in such a case, the aforesaid audit is undeniably characterized by both a national and a European dimension, which is a sample of the EU's intensive efforts for deeper cooperation and greater transparency as far as economic issues are concerned (European Court of Auditors, 2017).

Nonetheless, apart from the ECA, Union funds managed and spent by national authorities are subject to strict auditing by Supreme Audit Institutions in member states. As a final point, according to the fourth objective, ECA is a determining factor regarding the satisfactory implementation and development of international standards, such as those by INTOSAI (European Court of Auditors, 2017).

The European Ombudsman's noteworthiness is also fundamental, as he scrupulously investigates complaints about maladministration in Union's institutions and bodies. Emily O' Reilly, a distinguished author and journalist was elected as the European Ombudsman in July 2013, and took office on 1st October 2013. In December 2014, she was reelected for five more years (European Ombudsman, 2017; European Ombudsman/ CVs, 2017).

In the following chapter, an in-depth examination regarding

EU budget distribution takes place. The foremost processes are being meticulously analyzed and the most significant programs are being methodically evaluated.

In the difficult times we are currently experiencing with the economic crisis at international level and the unemployment nightmare, a critical view of EU budget distribution is absolutely necessary.

It has already been stressed that one of the dominant goals of this book is to enable the reader to draw fruitful conclusions about the rationale of the budget allocation, since the latter has occasionally provoked more than a few "heated", but concomitantly outstandingly interesting debates regarding its overall impact within the Union.

CHAPTER 3

EU BUDGET ALLOCATION

In the previous chapter, both the setting-up and the magnitude of EU budget were critically scrutinized. But what exactly was the Union budget for 2015 by heading of the financial framework? The reference to the budget can provide satisfactory answers to numerous important questions of economic nature.

The budget (commitments) thus took the following form: A) 46% in "Smart and inclusive growth" within the Union, subdivided into a) 34% for aid to both EU underdeveloped regions and the "disadvantaged" society sections and b) a rapid and efficient competitiveness strengthening as far as European firms are concerned[5], B) 41% in "Sustainable growth: natural resources", namely in a) sustainable land and forest use, b) optimal production of safe and secure food supplies, and c) innovative (and possibly far more effective) farming, C) 6% in "Administration", D) 6% in "Global Europe", E) 1% in "Security and citizenship" and F) lower percentages on "Compensations" and other special instruments (Europa/Budget, 2017).

---

5. *In other words, 34% was about "Economic, social and territorial cohesion", while 12% about "Competitiveness for growth and jobs".*

According to EU archives, in 2015, within the Union, some of the most vital programs and budgets were a) €10 bn for "Horizon 2020" program for research and innovation, b) €3.4 bn for Connecting Europe Facility (energy, transport and digital networks), c) €1.6 bn for Erasmus + (education, training, youth and sport), d) €1.4 bn for "Youth Employment Initiative", e) €0.4 bn for LIFE environmental program and f) €0.3 bn for COSME (small businesses) (Europa/Budget, 2017).

Particular attention must be paid to "Horizon 2020", which focuses on research and innovation and is one of the brightest hopes for EU's future development. Its principal objective is EU's progress in science and industry, as far as innovation is concerned (Europa/Budget, 2017; European Commission/Budget, 2014; HORIZON 2020/News, 2017; HORIZON 2020/What is Horizon 2020, 2017; Vasileiou, 2013a, 2013b, 2014a, 2014b, 2015 and 2017).

This way, the Union's notability at international level will be strengthened and critical issues such as a) food safety and security, b) climate change, c) a more efficient development of sustainable transport and mobility, d) cheap renewable energy and e) population aging will be successfully addressed (Europa/Budget, 2017; European Commission/Budget, 2014; HORIZON 2020/News, 2017; HORIZON 2020/What is Horizon 2020, 2017; Vasileiou, 2013a, 2013b, 2014a, 2014b, 2015 and 2017).

Concomitantly, this outstandingly significant program seeks the most effective link between research and the market, and in this direction it attempts to persuade innovative enterprises (based on their new technologies) to produce viable products with commercial success prospects (Europa/Budget, 2017; European Commission/Budget, 2014; HORIZON 2020/News, 2017; HORIZON 2020/What is Horizon 2020, 2017; Vasileiou, 2013a, 2013b, 2014a, 2014b, 2015 and 2017).

"Horizon 2020" is the financial instrument for the "Innovation Union" implementation, which is regarded as a cornerstone in terms of "Europe 2020", with the aim to guarantee Europe's worldwide competitiveness (Europa/Budget, 2017; European Commission/Budget, 2014; HORIZON 2020/News, 2017; HORIZON 2020/What is Horizon 2020, 2017; Vasileiou, 2013a, 2013b, 2014a, 2014b, 2015 and 2017).

It is worth highlighting that "Horizon 2020" possesses the (tremendously valuable) political support of not only European leaders, but also members of the European Parliament. They all firmly argue that research is a brilliant investment for a more positive future and should therefore be placed in the heart of the Union's blueprint for smart, sustainable and inclusive growth, as well as jobs (Europa/Budget, 2017; European Commission/ Budget, 2014; HORIZON 2020/News, 2017; HORIZON 2020/ What is Horizon 2020, 2017; Vasileiou, 2013a, 2013b, 2014a, 2014b, 2015 and 2017).

We argue that such a political support is entirely justified, since "Horizon 2020" is probably the Union's most noteworthy instrument for further development and for the successful confrontation regarding the nightmarish unemployment scourge. Moreover, this program aims at rapidly facilitating public-private cooperation for innovation enhancement in general (Europa/Budget, 2017; European Commission/Budget, 2014; HORIZON 2020/News, 2017; HORIZON 2020/What is Horizon 2020, 2017; Vasileiou, 2013a, 2013b, 2014a, 2014b, 2015 and 2017).

Apart from that, "Horizon 2020" is characterized by a relatively simple structure that systematically seeks to reduce bureaucracy. Furthermore, this program will be complemented by various significant measures with a view to completing and further developing the (equally crucial regarding future prospects) European Research Area (Europa/Budget, 2017; European Commission/Budget, 2014; HORIZON 2020/News, 2017; HORIZON 2020/What is Horizon 2020, 2017; Vasileiou, 2013a, 2013b, 2014a, 2014b, 2015 and 2017).

Special emphasis is placed on the fact that these measures will aim at removing all barriers towards the rapid establishment of an authentic single market for knowledge, research and innovation. The program's budget reaches €79.4 bn (Europa/Budget, 2017; European Commission/Budget, 2014; HORIZON 2020/News, 2017; HORIZON 2020/What is Horizon 2020, 2017; Vasileiou, 2013a, 2013b, 2014a, 2014b, 2015 and 2017).

At this point, it is essential to elucidate that budget distribution is by no means a strictly intra-Community issue. The Union as a major global partner has, inter alia, been tasked with numerous tremendously significant activities outside its borders, such as the maintenance of a lasting peace, the efficacious assistance to victims of conflicts or disasters and the methodical, as well as uninterrupted promotion of socioeconomic development (Europa/Budget, 2017).

These days that both the intense economic instability and the dangerous sociopolitical crises are a harsh reality, the EU multifarious role indubitably becomes even more critical.

Non-EU countries receiving funds from the Union budget are classified as follows: a) neighboring countries, namely those in Eastern Europe, the Middle East and North Africa, b) candidates or potential candidates to become EU members and c) certain parts of the developing world where some EU member states maintain historical ties (in particular regions in the Pacific, Africa and the Caribbean) (Europa/Budget, 2017).

Typical examples of programs outside EU in 2015 were a) the DCI (€2.4 bn), b) the "European Neighborhood Instrument" (€2 bn) and c) the Instrument for Pre-Accession Assistance (€1.6 bn) (Europa/Budget, 2017).

We will critically focus on DCI, which is indubitably a pivotal lever for further development, and poverty reduction is its fundamental pursuit. The entire spectrum of its objectives and general principles has been methodically prepared in accordance with Lisbon Treaty and latest policies, such as the "Agenda for Change". More specifically, DCI covers all developing countries, apart from those eligible for the Pre-Accession Instrument, through its different (but equally important) programs.

The main components covered are the following three: a) geographic programs, b) thematic programs, and c) the new "Pan-African Programme" (International Cooperation and Development, 2017).

In the context of geographic programs, fruitful cooperation with approximately 47 developing countries in Latin America, North, South, South East and Central Asia, the Middle East and South Africa is supported in the best possible manner (International Cooperation and Development, 2017).

In truth, these programs actually reinforce numerous remarkable actions based on the "European Consensus for Development", as well as the following categories: a) development and security, where conflict prevention is indeed included, b) resilience, coupled with appreciable disaster risk reduction, c) migration and asylum, d) sustainable and inclusive growth and development on burning issues, such as health, education, social protection, food security and sustainable agriculture, e) the link between humanitarian relief and development cooperation and f) good governance, human rights and democracy (International Cooperation and Development, 2017).

Literally, thematic programs benefit the entire range of developing countries, including those covered by the "European Neighborhood and Partnership Instrument" and the European Development Fund. They are divided into two categories. The first is the "Global Public Good and Challenges" program, which successfully addresses issues related to energy, the environment, food security, climate change, poverty reduction, migration and human development (International Cooperation and Development, 2017).

We focus on the fact that no less than 27% of the program is actually spent on environmental and climate change objectives, while at least 25% is used in order to effectively provide substantial support for human development and social inclusion. The second category is the "Civil society organisations and local authorities" program, which, as its name suggests, seeks to encourage both civil society and local authorities to play a more prominent role in the context of the (always important) development strategies (International Cooperation and Development, 2017).

Finally, the "Pan-African Programme" directly aims at an increased and intensified support and strengthening of the strategic partnership between Africa and the EU. As a matter of fact, it complements other financing instruments used in Africa and provides significant assistance as far as transregional, continental or worldwide activities both in Africa and with Africa are concerned (International Cooperation and Development, 2017).

More specifically, the budget allocated under the DCI for the period 2014-20 amounts to €19.6 bn and, in order to be more precise, €11.8 bn for geographic programs, €7 bn for thematic programs and €845 million for the "Pan-African Programme" (International Cooperation and Development, 2017).

Another key parameter that under no circumstances must go unnoticed is the fact that approximately 94% of EU budget funds real activities on the ground in both EU member states and non-EU countries. We argue that in more than a few cases, the budget is a primary aid instrument, not only for numerous regions, cities and non-governmental organizations, but also for thousands of researchers and millions of students (Europa/Budget, 2017; European Commission/Budget, 2014; Vasileiou, 2013a, 2013b, 2014a, 2014b, 2015 and 2017).

In addition to that, about 6% of the budget is earmarked for running costs, which include both administrative costs of all institutions and those for interpretation and translation in all the Union's official languages (Europa/Budget, 2017).

Emphasis is also placed on the staggering fact that the European Commission, as part of a reform package, reduces staffing by 1% per year, while increasing working hours. The aim is to finally achieve a 5% staff decrease (Europa/Budget, 2017), but only time will tell the feasibility of such an objective. It is clear that both staff reduction and working hours' increase are indubitably affected by political and economic developments, so the precise future workload is outstandingly difficult (if not impossible) to predict.

In Table 1 below, important information on the 2014-2020 MFF is being presented. "Sustainable growth: natural resources", "Economic, social and territorial cohesion" and "Competitiveness for growth and jobs" are at the top and are most likely to remain there beyond 2020 as well.

Table 1

MFF 2014-20/COMMITMENT APPROPRIATIONS [in million € (current prices)]		
MFF 2014-20	Million €	%
Sustainable growth: natural resources	420,034	38.9
Economic, social and territorial cohesion	366,791	33.9
Competitiveness for growth and jobs	142,130	13.1
Administration	69,584	6.4
Global Europe	66,262	6.1
Security and citizenship	17,725	1.6
Compensation	29	0.0
Source: European Commission/Budget, 2014.		

At this point, it is essential for a number of key Union programs to be scrupulously examined, since they are highly probable to substantially contribute to the rapid resolution of more than a few thorny problems.

The paramount "Human brain" project can in fact develop the most detailed model of brain analysis to date. It is based on the systematic and intensive use of specific supercomputing technologies and is considered to be revolutionary in the development of innovative forms and methods of treatment against brain diseases (European Commission/Budget, 2014).

What is more, the results may promote new and particularly interesting computing technologies. In the context of this program, numerous top-class European scientists take part and it is funded with €54 million by the Union (European Commission/ Budget, 2014).

Another remarkable initiative is the "Business Development Centre" at the Letterkenny Institute of Technology, which is situated in an Irish city in the country's north-west. This very city, with a population of approximately 20,000 people, has actually managed (with the Union's assistance) to turn into an outstandingly significant and highly sophisticated incubation, enterprise and research center called CoLab. The EU contributed €2.67 million (European Commission/Budget, 2014).

More specifically, 23 noteworthy business centers exist over 2,500 square meters and we would argue that this center is essentially serving as a significant incubator for start-ups, as it offers valuable facilities for industrial research. The aim is to provide entrepreneurs with the most effective support at every stage of their business development. The general philosophy of the Centre's operation made it famous and we must not ignore the fact that it currently has a momentous impact on the entire business community of northwest Ireland (European Commission/Budget, 2014).

The European Progress Microfinance Facility is another flawless establishment, since it is in charge of providing micro-loans (up to €25,000) to small enterprises as well as to people who have already lost or are in danger of losing their jobs and would like to create their own enterprise. We note that this mechanism is targeted at groups with limited access to conventional credit, namely disabled people, women, young people and minorities (European Commission/Budget, 2014).

It is worth mentioning that in 2013 the Union provided significant assistance to 124 million people in more than 90 countries outside EU, while making a real contribution to the systematic protection and promotion of human rights through a valuable joint EU and UNICEF project. Due to that remarkable project, between 2008 and 2011, the number of Senegalese villages quitting the practice of female genital mutilation increased from 300 to 5,315 which is a great achievement (European Commission/Budget, 2014).

Additionally, LIFE program, with a budget of €3.5 bn, successfully supports projects and activities relating to environmental protection, while RAPEX is an alert system for a rapid information exchange between the Commission and member states, aimed at reducing or totally preventing the marketing or use of products harmful to the consumers' health and safety (Europa/Budget, 2017; European Commission/ Budget, 2014; Vasileiou, 2013a, 2013b, 2014a, 2014b, 2015 and 2017).

MEDIA program manages to incessantly support both cinema and the EU audiovisual sector in general, with the aim of developing, distributing and promoting projects beyond national or European borders. COSME program is actively supporting SMEs, the competitiveness of which is a key Union priority (Europa/Budget, 2017; European Commission/Budget, 2014; Vasileiou, 2013a, 2013b, 2014a, 2014b, 2015 and 2017).

According to official 2014 EU figures, COSME would grant €2.3 bn to SMEs to enhance their competitiveness and maximize their growth and development of employment within Europe. Also, in the context of COSME, the so-called "zero bureaucracy" is being implemented in a remarkably effective manner, while the method of electronic reporting and submission, which greatly facilitates business, is being ceaselessly enhanced (Europa/Budget, 2017; European Commission/Budget, 2014; Vasileiou, 2013a, 2013b, 2014a, 2014b, 2015 and 2017).

Connecting Europe Facility is another noteworthy Union initiative since it aims to improve Europe's transport, energy and digital networks. Furthermore, it attempts to promote cleaner means of transport and fast broadband connections. Concurrently, it seeks to facilitate the use of energy from renewable sources and systematically works towards the rapid completion of internal energy market in order not only to ensure the highest possible security of supply for the EU, but also to reduce its energy dependency (Europa/Budget, 2017; European Commission/Budget, 2014; Vasileiou, 2013a, 2013b, 2014a, 2014b, 2015 and 2017).

The precise amount allocated to this facility reaches €33 bn and its value is demonstrated by the fact that it seeks to boost both employment and growth through cost-effective infrastructure investment, while, concomitantly, actively contributing towards environmental protection (Europa/Budget, 2017; European Commission/Budget, 2014; Vasileiou, 2013a, 2013b, 2014a, 2014b, 2015 and 2017).

Erasmus + program is responsible for youth, education, training and sport, with a view to enhancing both skills and employability. Its budget is approximately €15 bn and it is worth noting that it is increased by 40% compared to previous years (Europa/Budget, 2017; European Commission/Budget, 2014; Vasileiou, 2013a, 2013b, 2014a, 2014b, 2015 and 2017).

Such a raise is clearly revealing the Union's particular interest in young people. In particular, more than four million young people will receive significant support for study, training, work or voluntary work abroad (Europa/Budget, 2017; European Commission/Budget, 2014; Vasileiou, 2013a, 2013b, 2014a, 2014b, 2015 and 2017).

Of these, two million will be tertiary students, 650,000 vocational training college students, or apprentices and over 500,000 people taking part in youth exchanges, or volunteer work abroad. Additionally, up to 200,000 students planning a full-time postgraduate degree abroad will receive support by the European Investment Fund's new loan guarantee scheme. Finally, it is essential to underline that 600 sport partnerships will also be funded (European Commission/Budget, 2014; Vasileiou, 2013a, 2013b, 2014a, 2014b, 2015 and 2017).

The Asylum, Migration and Integration Fund, with a budget of €3.1 bn, appreciably enhances the satisfactory implementation in terms of a common approach to both asylum and immigration, and the functional management of migration flows (European Commission/Budget, 2014; Vasileiou, 2013a, 2013b, 2014a, 2014b, 2015 and 2017).

What is more, the Internal Security Fund, with a budget of €3.8 bn, not only fights crime and terrorism in a systematic and ceaseless manner, but also facilitates travel to the Union and ensures an adequate control level at external borders (European Commission/Budget, 2014; Vasileiou, 2013a, 2013b, 2014a, 2014b, 2015 and 2017).

In the following (and final) chapter, the foremost concluding remarks are being methodically summarized. We remain confident that the EU has thus far achieved a rational budget distribution based on the common interest (and given the present difficulties), but only time will tell the effectiveness of its strategies.

Nonetheless, as it has already been stated in the introduction, we deliberately choose to avoid any long-term considerations. The current fluidity makes any future forecast problematic, not only with regard to EU planning and policies but also to the majority of political or economic programs around the globe.

CHAPTER 4

CONCLUDING REMARKS

Our analysis chronologically extends from 1967, when the Union budget became a reality till these days. The foremost alterations, the most crucial political events, the occasional debates and the policies that have influenced the permanently complex strategies of the Union's budget between now and then have been meticulously scrutinized.

It is undisputed that the EU has been acting in the best possible manner in order for a fair budget distribution to be efficaciously achieved, towards the coveted targets of economic growth and social harmony. Nonetheless, several difficulties arising from the economic and financial crisis, combined with various sociopolitical tribulations must in no way be ignored, as they are incontrovertibly hampering progress.

Nevertheless, despite all difficulties that exist or may arise in the future, the Union continues to develop its strategies in a transparent manner and in the light of the specific needs of its citizens. Moreover, EU budget is an unambiguous proof of a profound European integration, and we indisputably support the fact that a strong and united Europe can provide numerous advantages and opportunities.

The principal conclusions drawn are four. Firstly, for the preparation and implementation of general policies and activities related to EU budget, a close and functional cooperation between the European Parliament, the Council of the EU, the European Commission, the ECA, the European Economic and Social Committee, the Committee of the Regions and the European Ombudsman is indubitably required. In order for positive results to be witnessed, such cooperation must be guided by intensified actions and excellent coordination.

Secondly, the Union has already ensured transparency in the decisions on spending modes and overall budgeting strategies. We avow that the entire range of procedures discussed in the previous chapters leave little doubt about this, since all "tools" available to the EU to efficaciously deal with fraud or maladministration have been methodically examined.

Thirdly, for 2015, 87% of the funds were allocated for a) "Smart and inclusive growth", including "Economic, social and territorial cohesion" and "Competitiveness for growth and jobs" and b) "Sustainable growth: natural resources". These are precisely the Union's dominant priorities and it is not difficult to understand why.

Fourthly, under the MFF 2014-20 (commitment appropriations), the aforementioned "Sustainable growth: natural resources", "Economic, social and territorial cohesion" and "Competitiveness for growth and jobs" are also of pivotal importance, due to the fact that burning issues such as a) economic, social and territorial cohesion via aid to the Union's underdeveloped regions and disadvantaged social groups, b) enterprises' competitiveness, c) production and food safety and d) the earth's efficient and sustainable use will probably remain key priorities even beyond 2020.

Apart from that, we have also acknowledged the unquestionably critical role of key components such as BUDG, CONT, Ecofin, Eurogroup, OLAF, ECO and ECON. The complexity of budget policies is such that systematic planning, maximum precision and emphasis on detail are incontrovertibly required.

Furthermore, programs, initiatives and funds, such as "Human brain", the "Business Development Centre" at the Letterkenny Institute of Technology, the European Progress Microfinance Facility, the joint EU and UNICEF project, LIFE, RAPEX, MEDIA, COSME, Connecting Europe Facility, Erasmus +, the Asylum, Migration and Integration Fund and the Internal Security Fund are unparalleled achievements, due to the fact that they have the potential to resolve more than a few burning problems and significantly improve the quality of life.

Additionally, particular emphasis was placed on both the paramount "Horizon 2020" program and DCI. "Horizon 2020" is considered to be one of the Union's main hopes for economic revival. Promotion of research and innovation in general, accompanied by the Union's further advancement in science and industry are irrefutably crucial, both for the present and the future.

Through "Horizon 2020", a steady optimism is detected that solutions regarding outstandingly critical issues namely unemployment, especially among young people, food safety, climate change and sustainable transport development can actually be found.

DCI performs equally noteworthy functions, since it is responsible for the gargantuan task of poverty reduction. Geographic programs, thematic programs, as well as the new "Pan-African Programme" seek to provide priceless assistance to the developing world in a multitude of flaming issues, including development, security, conflict prevention, migration, asylum, health, education, social protection, food security, sustainable agriculture, humanitarian assistance, democracy, good governance, energy, the environment and climate change.

Our critical analysis in the context of the abovementioned multidisciplinary programs, initiatives and mechanisms demonstrates in the most amiable way the Union's strong will for an optimized approach towards a wide range of activities, which is accompanied by a systematic method according to which its strategies are being designed.

Both via historical overviews and the meticulous examination of present conditions, we acknowledge not only the interdependence between EU institutions, but also the principal disagreements between member states and institutions that have periodically occurred. Such disputes may have resulted in severe tensions in the past, but we believe that in the majority of cases they eventually proved to be constructive, as they gave impetus in order for certain processes to be substantially improved. This practically led to a further strengthening of the budget's role in a wide range of particularly decisive issues.

We remain optimistic that through the text and the bibliography, the reader has been provided with a coherent understanding of the overall budget functioning, which essentially defines the entire Union's decision-making mechanism.

It would be utopian to attempt to precisely predict what the economic and sociopolitical future holds, as things are constantly changing at a rapid pace. Swift developments in a wide range of issues clearly affect the Union, which is often called upon to methodically adapt its policies in a specific manner in order to satisfactorily respond to precise needs and requirements.

We remain perfectly sure that at least for the time being, the EU has indeed succeeded in achieving a fair and efficient budget allocation so as to sufficiently cope with numerous pivotal issues, namely socioeconomic inequalities between countries and regions, food safety, fight against crime, climate change and respect for human rights.

BIBLIOGRAPHY

Cipriani, Gabriele (2014), *Financing the EU Budget-Moving Forward or Backwards? (Λονδίνο: Rowman & Littlefield International, Ltd.), available at https://www.ceps.eu/system/files/Financing%20 the%20EU%20budget_Final_Colour.pdf (accessed on 7/1/17).*

CoR Commissions (2017), *"Commission for Economic Policy-ECON" (in Greek), available at http://cor.europa.eu/el/activities/commissions/ Pages/cor-commissions.aspx?comm=ECON (accessed on 2/2/17).*

Europa/Budget (2017), *"Budget" (in Greek), available at https:// europa.eu/european-union/topics/budget_el (accessed on 4/1/17).*

Europa/How the EU budget is spent (2017), *"How the EU budget is spent" (in Greek), available at https://europa.eu/european- union/about-eu/money/expenditure_el (accessed on 4/2/17).*

Europa/How the EU is funded (2017). *"How the EU is funded" (in Greek), available at https://europa.eu/european-union/ about-eu/money/revenue-income_el (accessed on 4/2/17).*

Europa/Money and the EU (2017), *"Money and the EU" (in Greek), available at https://europa.eu/european- union/about-eu/money_el (accessed on 4/2/17).*

European Commission/Budget (2014), *"The European Union Explained- Budget" (in Greek), available at https://europa.eu/european-union/topics/ budget_el (the document is included in this webpage) (accessed on 5/1/17).*

European Council/Council of the European Union/Budget (2016), *"Budget of the EU" (in Greek), available at http://www.consilium. europa.eu/el/policies/eu-annual-budget/ (accessed on 31/1/17).*

European Council/Council of the European Union/Ecofin (2017), *"Economic and Financial Affairs Council configuration*

BIBLIOGRAPHY

(Ecofin)" (in Greek), available at http://www.consilium.europa.eu/ el/council-eu/configurations/ecofin/ (accessed on 31/1/17).

European Council/Council of the European Union/Eurogroup (2016), *"Eurogroup" (in Greek), available at http://www.consilium. europa.eu/el/council-eu/eurogroup/ (accessed on 1/2/17).*

European Court of Auditors (2017), *"European Court of Auditors, Guardians of the EU finances-ECA's Work" (in Greek), available at http:// www.eca.europa.eu/el/Pages/ECAWork.aspx (accessed on 30/1/17).*

European Economic and Social Committee (2017), *"Economic and Monetary Union and Economic and Social Cohesion (ECO)", available at http://www.eesc.europa.eu/?i=portal.en.eco-section (accessed on 2/2/17).*

European Ombudsman (2017), *"European Ombudsman" (in Greek), available at http://www.ombudsman.europa. eu/el/home.faces (accessed on 30/1/17).*

European Ombudsman/CVs (2017), *"CVs" (in Greek), available at http://www.ombudsman.europa.eu/el/ atyourservice/about-eo.faces (accessed on 30/1/17).*

European Parliament/Committees/Budgetary Control (2017), *"Budgetary Control-CONT" (in Greek), available at http://www.europarl. europa.eu/committees/el/cont/home.html (accessed on 30/1/17).*

European Parliament/Committees/Budgets (2017), *"Budgets-BUDG" (Jean Arthuis) (in Greek), available at http://www.europarl. europa.eu/committees/el/budg/home.html (accessed on 30/1/17).*

HORIZON 2020/News (2017), *"HORIZON 2020-The EU Framework Programme for Research and Innovation-Latest news and events", available at http://ec.europa.eu/ programmes/horizon2020/en/home (accessed on 14/2/17).*

BIBLIOGRAPHY

HORIZON 2020/What is Horizon 2020 (2017), "HORIZON
2020-The EU Framework Programme for Research and Innovation-
What is Horizon 2020?", available at http://ec.europa.eu/programmes/
horizon2020/en/what-horizon-2020 (accessed on 14/2/17).

Internal Audit Service (2017), "Service Department-IAS-
Internal Audit Service", available at https://ec.europa.eu/info/
departments/internal-audit-service (accessed on 2/2/17).

International Cooperation and Development (2017), "Development
Cooperation Instrument (DCI)", available at https://ec.europa.eu/europeaid/
funding/funding-instruments-programming/funding-instruments/
development-cooperation-instrument-dci_en (accessed on 14/2/17).

Matthijs, Herman (2010), "The Budget of the European
Union", Institute for European Studies, available at http://
www.ies.be/node/1062 (accessed on 7/2/17).

Nugent, Neill (2012), The Government and Politics of the European
Union (translated into Greek) (3rd fully revised edition) (Athens: Savvalas).

Núñez Ferrer, Jorge (2007), "The EU Budget-The UK Rebate
and the CAP-Phasing them both out?" CEPS Task Force Report
(Brussels: Centre for European Policy Studies), available at
http://aei.pitt.edu/9533/2/9533.pdf (accessed on 13/2/17).

OLAF (2017), "OLAF-European Anti-Fraud Office" (in Greek), available
at http://ec.europa.eu/anti-fraud/home_el (accessed on 2/2/17).

Seremetis, Dim. Vas. (1995), "The European Union Budget" in
Maravegias, Napoleon-Tsinisizelis Michalis (eds.) The European
Union Integration (in Greek) (Athens: Themelio), pp. 313-342.

BIBLIOGRAPHY

Vasileiou, Ioannis (2013a), *European Unification-A Process of Convergence, or Divergence? (in Greek) (Athens: Historical Quest).*

Vasileiou, Ioannis (2013b), *"1980-1999, European Union: The Years of Expansion and Enlargement", From Hitler's New Europe to Merkel's Eurozone (in Greek), Vol. 1, Historical Archive of Ependytis, pp. 76-95.*

Vasileiou, Ioannis (2014a), *European Unification-A Process of Convergence, or Divergence? (2nd Edition-Special Edition for Universities) (in Greek) (Athens: Historical Quest).*

Vasileiou, Ioannis (2014b), *The Present and Future of the Agricultural Policy of the European Union (in Greek) (Athens: Historical Quest).*

Vasileiou, Ioannis (2015), *The Foreign and Security Policy of the European Union-A Critical Approach (in Greek) (Athens: Historical Quest).*

Vasileiou, Ioannis (2017), *European Union and Energy-The Route Towards 2050-Thoughts, Ideas and Conclusions (in Greek) (Athens: Historical Quest).*

IOANNIS VASILEIOU

BIOGRAPHY

Ioannis Vasileiou was born in Athens in 1978. In 2001, he was awarded his Ptychio (equivalent to Bachelor's degree) in Political Science and Public Administration from the University of Athens (Greece). In 2003, he was awarded his first Master's degree (International Political Economy) from the University of Warwick (UK). In 2005, he was awarded his second Master's degree (International Economic Management) from the University of Birmingham (UK). In 2011, he was awarded his PhD from the University of Birmingham (UK) with specialization in the economic and political aspects of the European Union's Regional Policy. Since 2011, he has been conducting academic research on issues related to the European Union and international politics and economics.